oversized t-shirts
and overgrown pain

Ayana Abdulla

BookLeaf
Publishing

India | USA | UK

Presentation by *BookLeaf Publishing*

Web: www.bookleafpub.com

E-mail: info@bookleafpub.com

ISBN: 978-93-5744-983-0

First edition 2022

DEDICATION

For Nana

ACKNOWLEDGEMENT

I want to thank Aarav for staying up late, for many days, to edit, revise and inspire my writing. Thank you to Ms. Lora, Maya, and Carolina for editing, listening and supporting my work throughout this entire process. I want to thank BookLeaf for offering this opportunity to get my work into the world and hopefully impact even a small corner of it. I would finally like to thank my family for their support, love and willingness to share their stories. Thank you to everyone who made this dream possible.

PREFACE

All the context you'll need:
-Loss hurts so much more when you love
-The hurt will never go away but you'll learn to live again
-Grandfathers are the greatest role models and should be cherished endlessly

1.

Dear love,
You are my world.
You are my guide, my role model, my hero.
You showed me the importance of loving even
when no one wants to love back,
Laughing to the point that everyone thinks
you're crazy,
Admiring until I find value.
You showed me the beauty of life,
In the smallest insignificant moments.
And for that,
I forever thank you.
-for everything.

2.

I found it difficult to breathe.
Like the vines that invaded my grandfathers
lungs,
Slowly found their way into mine.

Their thorns made small slits into my sides,
Little by little,
So they'd go undetected.

So when I thought,
(Months from now, I'll be okay)
I had never spoken such wrong in my life.
For
Months from then,
The scratches would rip open my chest,
And a collection of thorned roses,
Chrysanthemum,
Dirt,
Bugs,
Vines,
Overtook my body,
Until it was no longer my own.
-homeless

3.

3

It's moments like this that make me doubt the
existence of God
-godless

4.

It occurred to me that you once asked,
(What will you do when I die?)
A little harsh for a couple of children to hear.
Nonetheless,
We respond with,
(Sit by your grave, everyday. So you would
never feel alone)

It occurred to me,
That if I want to go to university,
I should stay within the city so that I could visit
you after school and tell you about my day,
That if I wanted to have a family,
I should stay at home and just build upon the
one I already have,
That I should wait,
Because they may change their minds,
The gods,
The people,
The doctors…
And it occurred to me,
That I must stay.
-devoted

5.

I choose to believe in an afterlife,
Because if this is the way I react,
To knowing you're in a different world.
Then I don't want to know what it'll be like,
Knowing you're completely gone.
-shut eyes

6.

Today is supposed to be your birthday,
But all throughout the house,
Not a single phone rings,
Or a candle is blown out.
It's as if the rest of the world forgot.

It's funny because I remember the funeral.
Everyone holding me,
Telling me that they will never forget him,
And that they'd always be there for me.

I rummage through the drawers,
And grab a match,
Because that's all we have left,
And I put it in an old muffin,
And blow it out all alone.
I didn't forget,
I never will.
-Nobody cares anymore

7.

The only positive I've found throughout this
experience,
Is that death shows you who the real ones are.
-i'm surrounded by liars

8.

Looking back,
At almost any moment in my life,
I judge myself.
I think I've overreacted,
Made a fool.

But looking back,
And remembering you,
Your smile,
Your stories,
Your death,
I don't regret a thing I said,
Or heard.
I came to the realization that,
Regret and curiosity are two different things.
I wonder what would have happened if I did
something differently,
But the way it went,
Was worth the other mysteries.

Anyways,
Another universe,
Another me and you,
May have lived it out,
And they are thinking,

The exact same thing.
-universal

9.

I believe that every action,
Triggers another.
Everything we do,
Affects the entirety of the rest of our lives.
Which always leaves me thinking,
If I said something differently,
If I didn't go to my cousins house that weekend,
Or if I woke up an hour later in my grandma's
bed,
Or if I didn't tell myself that I wanted you to be
free,
That maybe it wouldn't have happened,
And maybe you'd still be here with me.
-the caterpillar effect

10.

When I perform,
Walk down the aisle,
Graduate from high school,
I'll look into the audience,
For your eyes,
And smile,
And proud face,
But never find it.
-missing

11.

Despite what they tell you,
Grief is not a five stage process.
It flips and turns,
It progresses slowly,
And sometimes too fast to keep up.
Some days,
I drop all the way back to the beginning,
And I can't stop thinking.
Others,
I skip all the way till the end,
Till I'm healed,
And I can hardly think at all.
-growth is messy

12.

And although it was hard,
He saved me.
Not like the whole knight in shining armour,
And damsel in distress.

More like a caretaker,
Looking after his little plants.
-some light in all the dark

13.

It was that morning,
The one with sun,
And light wind,
The 'perfect' day.

My home,
My safe place,
Invaded by hundreds of people.
I felt like I was being pushed around a busy
street in New York.
Except everyone was looking at me,
And hugging me,
And kissing my forehead.
That lasted for about a week,
And after that,
My street emptied,
And those kisses,
Words of wisdom,
Endless love,
Disappeared.
It's like they think grief only lasts a week.
-it's still here

14.

You're never going to watch me grow up,
But don't worry,
When we reunite,
The story will finish,
This is just the intermission.
-my life is a theatrical performance

15.

The day you died I lost more than just you.
I lost my grandfather,
My protection,
My happiness,
My ability to love,
My voice,
My faith,
Myself,
I lost myself.
-all that's worth living for is no longer alive

16.

You were the only one that could tell me I was
beautiful and I'd believe it.
-dead beauty

17.

As you rest peacefully,
I wish to see what's left of the world,
So I may come back and tell you everything you
missed.
I want to live my life on your behalf.
-leaving

18.

I now understand,
That no matter how far I go,
We will always be sheltered by the same sky,
Call the same place home,
And love the same way.

No matter how far I go,
You will always be with me,
In my heart,
My mind,
My smile,
My laugh.
-remembrance day is everyday

19.

And although I didn't believe in god,
Every night before I went to bed,
I prayed,
And I prayed,
And I prayed,
Until I knew,
That if I prayed anymore,
God would punish me for the disturbance.
-evil angels

20.

The pain is still there,
But the hollow degrading vines that once
invaded my lungs,
Slowly wilted,
And were replaced with flowers,
Endless petals for which I lived by.

I used to take my breath for granted,
But I never want to know what it was like,
To lay all alone in that hospital bed,
And run out of petals.
-restricted

21.

When I get a copy of this story, our story,
I will drive to your home,
To where you rest,
And I will read the words that I can hardly type,
I will read the words that I can't bring myself to
look at,
In hopes that you will remember,
Even a little of the amount you affected me
-thank you for everything